NATIONAL GEOGRAPHIC

Kids Connect

PATHFINDER EDITION

By Kent Page, Terrell Smith, and Peter Winkler

CONTENTS

The sun has not yet risen over the rocky hills outside the city of Peshawar, in Pakistan. Loudspeakers from the top of a mosque (MAHSK), or Muslim house of worship, call out to the people, “God is great! It is better to pray than sleep! Come to prayers!”

Ten-year-old Garana rises from a mat on the floor of her family’s house. She puts on her black robe and covers her head with an old shawl. Then she walks to the mosque to pray.

Garana and her family have lived in their one-room house for several years. It’s one of thousands of homes made of mud-brick in the Shamshatoo Afghan **Refugee** Camp. The camp holds about 50,000 Afghan refugees. They are people who have fled from war or drought in Afghanistan.

Garana works hard. Her father left the family several years ago. Her mother can’t see very well and can do little to help. Her older brother works all day weaving carpets. And her younger brother is too small to do many chores. So Garana does most of the household tasks. But her day is not all work. She has time for school and even a little fun.

A day in the life of a young Afghan refugee

Garana's Story

BY KENT PAGE

Home Away from Home. *Garana lives in this refugee camp in Pakistan. Her family fled from war-torn Afghanistan several years ago.*

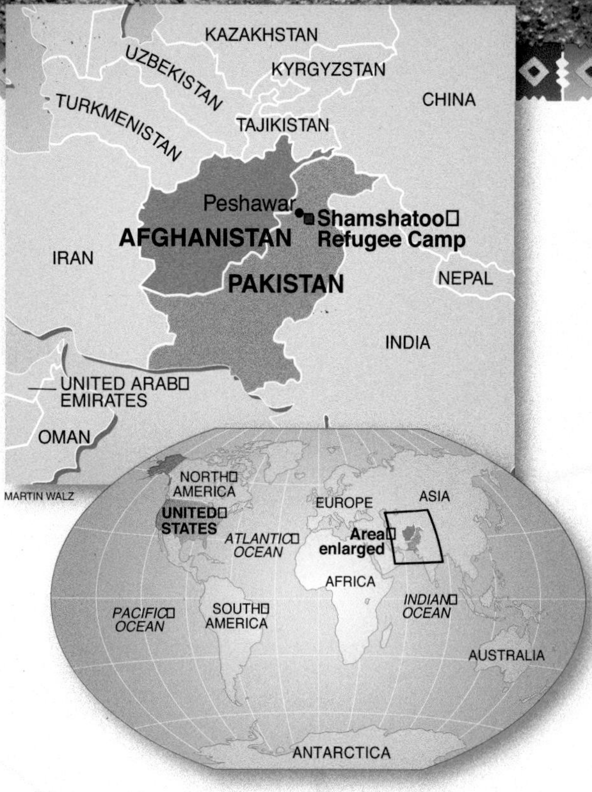

Weighty Experience. *Garana fetches water for her family. She uses the full weight of her body to move the pump handle*

Follow the Letters. *Garana and her teacher guide the class through the English alphabet.*

Early Morning

After prayers, Garana begins her morning chores. She walks to the camp's water pump to fill two bottles. After bringing them home, she eats breakfast, which is usually hot tea and bread. Then she washes the dishes in the backyard, using cold water from the pump. Next she sweeps the floor of the one-room house.

Then it's time to walk to the bakery. There she leaves a small amount of flour. The bakers will use it to make a loaf of bread. Garana's family will eat that loaf for their next three meals.

Now it's time to walk to school.

Class Time

Children in the refugee camp go to school six days a week. Boys and girls **attend** separate classes. Garana is in first grade, although she is ten years old. That's because when she lived in Afghanistan, Garana and the other girls were not allowed to go to school.

Garana has a lot of catching up to do. Classes in Garana's school go only through the second grade for girls and the third grade for boys. Still, it's an important start.

Bread Bakers. *Every day Garana takes some flour to the bakers. They use it to make bread for her family.*

Garana gets to school just before classes begin at 8:30. The concrete building has six classrooms. These rooms have no windows, but there is paint on the walls.

Thirty-five girls are in Garana's class. The students sit on mats on the floor. They study mathematics, the Afghan languages of Pashto and Dari, and the English alphabet. There is also class time for singing and drawing. Garana enjoys school.

"My favorite subject is English," she says. "If you can speak languages, then you can understand what people are saying. It's easier to get things done."

Today Garana stands at the chalkboard with a ruler and leads the class through the English alphabet. She mixes up *b* and *d*. Otherwise, she recites the alphabet perfectly.

Lunch Break

Classes end before lunch. The students race out to the small dirt playground to play on the swings, the slide, and the merry-go-round. Garana usually visits with her friends. But soon it's time for more chores.

She heads to the bakery to pick up the bread. Then she walks along the narrow streets to her house. After a quick hello to her mother, Garana goes to the pump to collect water. When she returns, she fills the teapot and puts it on the small stove.

Garana sits on her mat and eats her lunch. Today her mother has prepared potatoes along with the bread and tea.

"Some days we have potatoes. Some days we have rice. And some days we have beans," Garana says. "Whatever we eat for lunch, we have again for dinner. Rice is my favorite food."

Afternoon and Evening

After lunch, Garana heads back to the pump for water to wash the plates and cups. Then she sweeps the house, cleans the yard, and feeds the family's four chickens. Once in a while, when there is money, she goes to the local shop to buy food. After she finishes her chores, she does her homework.

Soon it's time for dinner. Because the houses in the refugee camp have no electricity, the family eats the evening meal before it gets dark. Then, if any daylight is left, Garana plays with her best friend, Assia.

A Wish for Peace

Garana has a hard life in the refugee camp. But at least there is no fighting. "I would like to go back to Afghanistan," she says, "but not until there is **peace** everywhere. We are told at school that some parts of Afghanistan are safe. But there is still fighting in other parts."

Many others share Garana's wish. For more than 30 years, the nation has suffered from war and unrest. Now the Afghan people, with the help of countries around the world, are trying to make changes. They hope to bring peace to Afghanistan.

Wordwise

attend: to go to a place regularly

donate: to give as a gift

peace: when there is no war or suffering

refugee: a person forced to leave home and go to live in another country

High Hopes. *Garana and Assia (in pink shirt) dream of returning to the mountains of Afghanistan.*

Back to School

Education = Hope for Afghan Children

By Terrell Smith

It was March 25, 2002. Crowds of boys and girls gathered throughout Afghanistan. Excited whispers filled the air. Many children had waited and waited for this moment. The first day of school was about to begin!

Were these children really that happy to start school? The answer is yes. Many Afghan children hadn't attended school in years. Girls weren't allowed to go. And staying home seemed safer for some boys.

Ready to Learn. *Afghan students hold new school supplies donated by kids in the United States.*

Without schools, many Afghan children were growing up without the skills they needed to earn a living. They faced lives of poverty. So, for them, school equals hope.

Class Acts

Unfortunately, years of fighting had destroyed or damaged 2,000 Afghan schools. The rest were in poor shape. And no one had money or materials to fix them.

So the United Nations Children's Fund (UNICEF) and the American Red Cross pitched in. Working with Afghan leaders, they repaired broken windows and doors. They also bought new desks, chairs, chalkboards, and textbooks.

U.S. students helped, too. They **donated** money that paid for chests full of school supplies. Afghan students got pencils, chalk, crayons, notebooks, rulers, jump ropes, and soccer balls.

No Complaints

All this help was just a start. Afghan schools still don't have space for every student. Classrooms are cramped, and tents hold extra classes.

To ease crowding, most schools have two shifts. Half the children attend morning classes. The other half go in the afternoon. But Afghan students aren't complaining. They're just glad to be back.

"I never stopped thinking about the day when I might go back to school," says Safi, a nine-year-old girl. "And then one day I heard on the radio that school would start again. I was so happy."

Making Fri

By Peter Winkler

"Enemies" learn and play together at Israel's Hand in Hand School. Now can they teach their parents how to live in peace?

Each morning in Israel, 300 kids do something extraordinary: They go to school. What's the big deal? Well, their schools mix Palestinians and Jews—peacefully. The two groups, Palestinians and Jews, have fought for decades. Violence has torn the country apart.

Differences between the two groups are so deep that Israel's two populations rarely meet. Jews and Palestinians generally live in different areas. They don't share a language or a religion, and their children attend separate schools.

Bridging differences like these can seem impossible. But two friends have decided to try.

Who's Who? *One student is Palestinian and the other two students are Jewish. Yet they laugh together like any group of friends.*

ends

Mission Impossible?

Lee Gordon is Jewish and Amin Khalaf is Palestinian. They met each other in 1996 and they formed an **organization** called Hand in Hand. Its **mission** is to build schools where Palestinians and Jews can be classmates—and friends.

What is it like to attend such an unusual school? Let's visit Jerusalem, Israel's capital, to find out.

Learning Shalom

On school days, the kids start showing up around 7:30 a.m. They greet the guard and then walk through a metal gate. Security is a big issue in Israel. One morning, for example, a teacher arrived late, crying and shaking. When she was driving to work, she saw a bus explode before her eyes.

Such events remind students and teachers how important their school is. "Every time a bombing occurs, we talk about it in class," says a Palestinian student. The kids discuss how hatred can lead to tragedy. Then they explore better ways to solve Israel's problems.

"If there were more schools like this," explains a Jewish friend, "then more children would learn shalom [peace]. They would grow up to be peaceful."

Teaching by Example. *A Palestinian teacher talks with her students. Jewish and Palestinian teachers work together at the Hand in Hand Schools.*

Speaking My Language

Soon it's 8:15 a.m. and time to start class. It's time to learn shalom—in two languages.

Roughly half the students are Jewish, and they speak Hebrew, the official language of Israel. The other half are Palestinians, and they speak Arabic. So how do the teachers decide which language to use? Hand in Hand's answer is to use both.

How? Each class has two teachers. One teaches in Arabic, while the other teaches in Hebrew. They plan and teach lessons together.

What they *don't* do is translate what the other is saying. So kids must listen in both of the languages. It's not easy, but students catch on quickly. By third grade, most students at Hand in Hand are **bilingual**. That means they know two languages.

What languages do the students use for writing? That depends. Sometimes the teachers tell students to write in Hebrew and sometimes in Arabic. At other times, the kids get a choice.

Classes end at 1:30 p.m., but the learning doesn't stop. It continues.

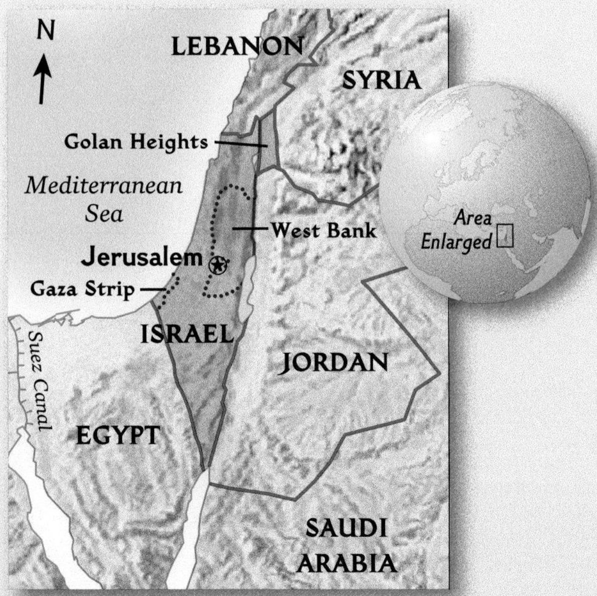

Busy Street. *Palestinian kids watch soldiers patrolling a street.*

Bridging Differences

After five hours of classes, everyone's eager for lunch. The school provides meals for everybody. The cooks follow food-related rules from the students' religions.

Once lunch is over, it's activity time. Students might try karate or yoga. They can play soccer, practice music, or design books. True to the school's focus on understanding other cultures, there's even a class in origami—the Japanese art of folding paper.

Afternoon activities don't sound as serious as math or science. But casual times together are an important part of a Hand in Hand education. Through these activities, students learn to see each other as ordinary people. They form friendships that bridge real, deep differences.

School wraps up at 3:30 p.m., and the kids head home. There the students become the teachers.

Home Schooling

"My Palestinian friends always ask me about school," says a student. Neighborhood kids can't imagine going to school with Jews. So they ask all kinds of things. "Don't they scare you? Don't they yell at you? Aren't they mean to you?" Jewish classmates get similar questions from their neighbors and relatives.

Hand in Hand students, Palestinian or Jewish, give pretty much the same answer. It goes a bit like this: "No, I'm not afraid. They're good people. They're my friends. I wish you could come to my school and see for yourself."

Like kids everywhere, Hand in Hand students bring friends home. Those friends may be the first Jews or Palestinians the rest of the family ever gets to know. Having an "enemy" in the house is uncomfortable—at first. Soon, though, people are eating together, talking together, playing together.

One friendship at a time, they're learning shalom.

Wordwise

bilingual: able to use two languages

bridge: to make connections between

mission: the goal or purpose of an organization

organization: an official group that works for a common goal

Make a Difference!

Answer these questions about the ways kids can connect with others.

1. What household tasks does Garana do to help her family?

2. What is Garana's favorite subject in school? Why does she like it?

3. How have students in the U.S. helped students in Afghanistan?

4. How do Hand in Hand School students use activities to bridge differences?

5. What do Hand in Hand School students do after classes? How does the author organize the events that take place at school?